How do I use this scheme?

Key Words with Peter and Jane has three
parallel series, each containing twelve books. All three
series are written using the same carefully controlled
vocabulary. Readers will get the most out of **Key Words** with
Peter and Jane when they follow the books in the pattern
1a, 1b, 1c; 2a, 2b, 2c and so on.

• Series a
gradually introduces and repeats new words.

• Series b
provides further practice of these same words, but
in a different context and with different illustrations.

• Series c
uses familiar words to teach **phonics** in a methodical way,
enabling children to read increasingly difficult words.
It also provides a link to writing.

LADYBIRD BOOKS

UK | USA | Canada | Ireland | Australia
India | New Zealand | South Africa

Ladybird Books is part of the Penguin Random House group of companies
whose addresses can be found at global.penguinrandomhouse.com.

www.penguin.co.uk   www.puffin.co.uk   www.ladybird.co.uk

First published 1964
This edition 2009, 2014, 2016
Copyright © Ladybird Books Ltd, 1964
001

A CIP catalogue record for this book is
available from the British Library

ISBN: 978-1-409-30142-4

Printed in China

Key Words

with Peter and Jane

12c The open door to reading

written by W. Murray
illustrated by J.H. Wingfield, F. Hampson
and R. Embleton

The publishers are very grateful for permission given to reprint copyright material from the following books :—

'THE LITTLE BOOKROOM' by Eleanor Farjeon.
Published by Oxford University Press.

'NICHOLAS NYE' by Walter de la Mare
by permission of The Literary Trustees of Walter de la Mare and The Society of Authors as their representative.

'HOW THE WHALE GOT HIS THROAT' by Rudyard Kipling, from the 'JUST SO STORIES' by permission of Mrs. George Bambridge and Macmillan & Co. Ltd. (British Commonwealth and Empire) and Doubleday and Company, Inc. (U.S.A.)

'SWALLOWS AND AMAZONS' by Arthur Ransome.
Published in Great Britain by Jonathan Cape Ltd. and in the United States by J. B. Lippincott Company.

'NORDY BANK' by Sheena Porter.
Published by Oxford University Press.

Contents

THE LITTLE BOOKROOM

by Eleanor Farjeon

In the home of my childhood there was a room we called 'The Little Bookroom'. True, every room in the house could have been called a bookroom. Our nurseries upstairs were full of books. Downstairs my father's study was full of them. They lined the dining-room walls, and overflowed into my mother's sitting-room, and up into the bedrooms.

Of all the rooms in the house, the Little Bookroom was yielded up to books as an untended garden is left to its flowers and weeds. There was no selection or sense of order here. In dining-room, study, and nursery there was choice and arrangement; but the Little Bookroom gathered to itself a motley crew of strays and vagabonds, outcasts from the ordered shelves below, the overflow of parcels bought wholesale by my father in the sales-rooms. Much trash, and more treasure. Riff-raff and gentle folk and noblemen. A lottery, a lucky dip for a child who had never been forbidden to handle anything between covers.

Crammed with all sorts of reading, the narrow shelves rose halfway up the walls; their tops piled with untidy layers that almost touched the ceiling. The heaps on the floor had to be climbed over, columns of books flanked the window, toppling at a touch. You tugged at a promising binding, and left a new surge of literature underfoot; and you dropped the book that had attracted you for something that came to the surface in the up-heaval. Magic casements opened for me through which I looked out on other worlds and times than those I lived in: worlds filled with poetry and prose and fact and fantasy.

Here, in the Little Bookroom, I learned, like Charles Lamb, to read anything that can be called a book.

The Lovebirds

(An extract from ' The Little Bookroom')

Whenever a child came to buy a penny fortune, Old
Dinah, the gypsy, said, "Put your finger in the cage,
Ducky!" And when the child did so, one of the two
lovebirds hopped on to the finger and was brought out
with a flutter of wings. Then Old Dinah held out the
fortunes in a little packet of folded papers, pink, and
green, and purple, and blue, and yellow, that always
hung outside the cage-door. And the wonderful lovebird
picked out one of the fortunes with its curved beak,
and the child took it. But just how did the lovebird know
which was the right fortune for the right child — the
right one for Marion, for Cyril, for Helen, for Hugh?
All the children put their heads together over the little
coloured papers, and wondered.

"What's *your* fortune, Marion?"

"I'm to marry a King. It's a purple one. What's *yours*,
Cyril?"

"A green one. I'm to go on a long journey. What's
Helen's?"

"I got a yellow one," said Helen, "and I'm to have
seven children. What's *your* fortune, Hugh?"

"I'm to succeed in all my undertakings. It's blue,"
said Hugh.

Susan Brown listened with all her ears. How beautiful
to have a fortune! If only she had a penny to spare!
But Susan Brown was very poor. She never had a penny
to spare, and not often any other sort of penny either.

But one day, when the other children had gone, and
Old Dinah was nodding in the sun, something lovely
happened. The door of the lovebirds' cage had been
left open a little by accident, and one of them got out.
Old Dinah, asleep in her chair, didn't see. But Susan
saw what happened.

Susan saw the little green bird hop from its perch and flutter to the pavement. She saw it run along the kerb a little way, and she saw a thin cat crouch in the gutter. Susan's heart gave such a jump that it made her body jump too. She jumped before the cat did, and ran across the road crying, "Shoo!"

The cat turned away as though it were thinking of something else, and Susan put her hand down to the lovebird, and the lovebird hopped on to her finger. Now to have a lovebird sitting on your finger is as lovely a thing as anyone can wish for on a summer day; it was the loveliest thing that had happened to Susan Brown in all her life. But that wasn't all, for just as they got to the cage-door the lovebird stretched out its beak, and picked a rose-pink fortune from the packet, and gave it to Susan. She couldn't believe it was true, but it was. She put the lovebird in the cage, and went off with her fortune in her hand.

In time Marion and Cyril and Helen and Hugh stopped going to school. They had lost their fortunes long ago and forgotten all about them. And Marion married the chemist's young man, and Cyril sat all day in an office, and Helen never happened to marry at all, and Hugh never happened to do anything whatever.

But Susan Brown kept her fortune all her life. By day she kept it in her pocket, and by night she kept it under her cheek. She didn't know what was in it, because she couldn't read. But it was a rose-pink fortune, and she hadn't had to buy it — it had been given to her.

BLACK BEAUTY

(Adapted from Anna Sewell's book ' Black Beauty ' — a famous animal story written as though by a horse. It tells of the days before motor cars when horses were used.)

The first place that I can well remember was a large pleasant meadow with a pond of clear water in it. Some trees overshadowed the pond, and rushes and water lilies grew at the deep end. Over the hedge on one side we looked into a ploughed field; and on the other, we looked over a gate at our master's house which stood by the roadside. At the top of the meadow was a plantation of fir-trees, and at the bottom, a running brook overhung by a steep bank.

Whilst I was young I lived upon my mother's milk, as I could not eat grass. In the daytime I ran by her side and at night I lay down close by her. When it was hot, we used to stand by the pond in the shade of the trees.

As soon as I was old enough to eat grass, my mother used to go out to work in the daytime, and to come back in the evening. There were six young colts in the meadow besides me. I used to run with them, and have great fun. Sometimes we had rather rough play.

One day, when there was a good deal of kicking, my mother said to me, "You have been well bred and well born, and I think you have never seen me kick or bite. I hope you will grow up gentle and good, and never learn bad ways. Do your work with a good will; and lift up your feet well when you trot, and never bite or kick even in play." I have never forgotten my mother's advice.

(Fire in the stables — an exciting extract from a later part of the book.)

The trap door had been left open, and I thought that was the place from which the smoke came. I listened and heard a soft, rushing sort of noise, and a low crackling and snapping. I did not know what it was, but there was something in the sound so strange that it made me tremble all over. The other horses were now all awake; some were pulling at their halters, others were stamping.

Danger seemed to be all around; there was nobody whom we knew to trust in, and all was strange and uncertain. The fresh air that had come in through the open door made it easier to breathe, but the rushing sound overhead grew louder, and as I looked upward, through the bars of my empty rack, I saw a red light flickering on the wall. Then I heard a cry of "Fire!" outside, and the old ostler came quietly and quickly in. He got one horse out, and went to another; but the flames were playing round the trap door, and the roaring overhead was dreadful.

The next thing I heard was James's voice, quiet and cheery, as it always was. "Come, my beauties, it is time for us to be off, so wake up and come along." I stood nearest the door, so he came to me first, patting me as he came in.

"Come, Beauty, on with your bridle, my boy, we'll soon be out of this smother." It was on in no time; then he took the scarf off his neck, and tied it lightly over my eyes, and, patting and coaxing, he led me out of the stable. Safe in the yard, he slipped the scarf off my eyes, and shouted, "Here, somebody! Take this horse while I go back for the other."

TREASURE ISLAND

(Adapted from R. L. Stevenson's ' Treasure Island' — Young Jim Hawkins, the hero of ' Treasure Island', was alone with the wounded coxswain (Israel Hands) on the drifting ship 'Hispaniola'. Everyone else was on shore. Jim tells how the wounded pirate tried to kill him.)

I thought that Hands could not move, because of his wound. He sat on the deck nursing his hurt leg, drinking brandy and saying what an unlucky ship the 'Hispaniola' was. Then he told me to go below to the cabin for him.

"You get me a bottle of wine, Jim—this here brandy's too strong for my head," the coxswain said. But he spoke in a strange way that made me suspicious. He seemed guilty and embarrassed, and I believed he wanted me to leave the deck. I could not imagine why. However, I did not let him see my suspicions.

"Some wine?" I said. "Far better. Will you have white or red?"

"Well, I reckon it's about the blessed same to me, shipmate," he replied, "if it's strong and there's plenty of it, what's the odds?"

I scuttled down the companion way with all the noise I could, slipped off my shoes, ran quietly along the sparred gallery, mounted the forecastle ladder, and popped my head out of the fore companion. I knew he would not expect me there, yet I was careful that he did not see me.

My worst suspicions proved true. Hands had moved across the deck to the port scuppers. There he picked, out of a coil of rope, a long knife discoloured to the hilt with blood. He tried its point upon his hand, then he hid the knife in his jacket and moved hastily back to his old place against the bulwark. He did not want me to know that he had moved, or that he had a knife.

(Later, Jim Hawkins was steering the ship and realized he was in danger.)

I was so much interested, waiting for the ship to touch, that I had quite forgot the peril that hung over my head. I might have fallen without a struggle for my life, had not a sudden disquietude seized upon me, and made me turn my head.

Perhaps I had heard a creak, or seen his shadow moving with the tail of my eye; perhaps it was an instinct like a cat's; but sure enough, when I looked round, there was Hands, already half-way towards me, with the knife in his right hand.

We must both have cried out aloud when our eyes met; but while mine was the shrill cry of terror, his was a roar of fury like a charging bull's. At the same instant he threw himself forward, and I leapt sideways towards the bars. As I did so, I left hold of the tiller. I think this saved my life, for it struck Hands across the chest, and stopped him, for the moment, dead.

Before he could recover, I was safe out of the corner where he had me trapped, with all the deck to dodge about. Wounded as he was, it was wonderful how fast Hands could move, his grizzled hair tumbling over his face, and his face itself red with haste and fury.

One thing I saw plainly: I must not simply retreat before him, or he would speedily hold me boxed into the bars, as a moment since he had so nearly boxed me in the stern. Once so caught, and nine or ten inches of the bloodstained knife would be my last experience on this side of eternity. I placed my palms against the mainmast, which was of a goodish bigness, and waited, every nerve upon the stretch.

I had to find some new way of escape at once, for my foe was almost touching me. Quick as thought I sprang into the mizzen shrouds, rattled up hand over hand, and did not draw a breath till I was seated on the cross-trees. I had been saved by being quick; the knife had struck not half a foot below me, as I climbed up; and there stood Hands, with his mouth open and his face upturned to mine, a picture of surprise and disappointment.

Now that I had a moment to myself, I lost no time in changing the priming of my pistol, and then having one ready for use, to make doubly sure, I proceeded to re-charge the other.

Hands began to see the dice going against him. Then, after hesitating, he also hauled himself heavily into the shrouds, and with the knife between his teeth, began slowly and painfully to mount, hauling his wounded leg behind him.

"One more step, Mr. Hands," said I, "and I'll blow your brains out!" He stopped instantly. I could see by the working of his face that he was trying to think. In order to speak he took the dagger out of his mouth.

"Jim," said he, "I reckon we're fouled, you and me, and we'll have to sign articles." Then, all in a breath, back went his right hand over his shoulder. Something sang like an arrow through the air; I felt a blow and then a sharp pang, and there I was pinned by the shoulder to the mast. In the horrid pain and surprise of the moment both my pistols went off and both escaped out of my hands.

They did not fall alone; with a choked cry, the coxswain loosed his grasp upon the shrouds, and plunged head first into the water.

NICHOLAS NYE
by Walter de la Mare

Thistle and darnel and dock grew there,
And a bush, in the corner, of may,
On the orchard wall I used to sprawl
In the blazing heat of the day;
Half asleep and half awake,
While the birds went twittering by,
And nobody there my lone to share
But Nicholas Nye.

Nicholas Nye was lean and grey,
Lame of a leg and old,
More than a score of donkey's years
He had seen since he was foaled;
He munched the thistles, purple and spiked,
Would sometimes stoop and sigh,
And turn his head, as if he said,
"Poor Nicholas Nye!"

Alone with his shadow he'd drowse in the meadow,
Lazily swinging his tail,
At break of day he used to bray—
Not much too hearty and hale;
But a wonderful gumption was under his skin,
And a clean calm light in his eye,
And once in a while, he'd smile—
Would Nicholas Nye.

THE STORY OF THUMBELINA

by Hans Andersen

Once upon a time, a beggar woman went to the house of a poor peasant, and asked for something to eat. The peasant's wife gave her some bread and milk. When she had eaten it, she took a barley-corn out of her pocket, and said, "This I will give to you; set it in a plant-pot, and see what you will get out of it."

The woman set the barley-corn in an old plant-pot, and the next day the most beautiful plant had shot up, which looked just like a tulip, but the petals were shut close together as if it were still in bud.

"What a pretty flower it is!" said the woman, and kissed the small red petals; and just as she had kissed them, the flower gave a great crack and opened itself. It was a real tulip, only one could see that in the middle of the flower there sat a tiny little girl, so delicate and lovely and not half so big as my thumb. So the woman called her Thumbelina.

A pretty polished walnut-shell was her cradle, blue violet-leaves were her mattress, and a rose-leaf was her coverlet. Here she slept at night, but during the day she played upon the table, where the woman had set a bowl, around which she placed quite a garland of flowers, the stalks of which were put in water. A large tulip-leaf floated on the water. Thumbelina seated herself on this, and sailed from one end of the bowl to the other; she had two white horse-hairs with which to row her little boat. It looked quite lovely; and she sang, oh! so beautifully.

(Later, Thumbelina sails away on a water-lily leaf.)

Thumbelina sailed past a great many places, and the little birds sitting in the bushes looked at her and sang, "What a pretty little maiden!" The leaf on which she stood floated away farther and farther, and at last she came to a foreign land.

A pretty, white butterfly stayed with her and flew about her. At length it seated itself upon the leaf, for by now it knew Thumbelina quite well, She was very pleased, because now she knew that the frog could not come near her, and the land to which she had come was very beautiful. The sun shone upon the water, and it was like the most lovely gold. She took off her girdle, and bound one end of it to the butterfly, and the other end of it to the leaf. In this way she glided on more swiftly than ever, and she stood upon the leaf as it went.

As she was sailing along so charmingly, a large stag-beetle came flying towards her; it paused for a moment to look at her, then clasped its claws round her slender waist, and flew up into a tree with her; but the green lily-leaf floated downstream, and the white butterfly with it, because it was fastened to it, and could not get loose.

Poor Thumbelina! how frightened she was when the stag-beetle flew away with her up into a tree! But she was most of all distressed because she had fastened the lovely white butterfly to the leaf and it could not get loose. But that did not trouble the stag-beetle at all. It seated itself upon one of the largest green leaves of the tree, gave her the honey of the flowers to eat, and said, "You are very pretty, although you are not at all like a stag-beetle."

THE PIED PIPER OF HAMELIN

(By Robert Browning — The town of Hamelin was over-run with rats and the Mayor and Council were wondering how to get rid of them.)

"Come in!"—the Mayor cried, looking bigger:
And in did come the strangest figure.
His queer long coat from heel to head
Was half of yellow and half of red;
And he himself was tall and thin;
With sharp blue eyes, each like a pin,
And light, loose hair, yet swarthy skin,
No tuft on cheek nor beard on chin,
But lips where smiles went out and in;
There was no guessing his kith and kin:
And nobody could enough admire
The tall man and his quaint attire.

He advanced to the council-table;
And "Please your honours," said he, "I'm able,
By means of a secret charm, to draw
All creatures living beneath the sun,
That creep or swim or fly or run,
After me so as you never saw!
And I chiefly use my charm
On creatures that do people harm,
The mole and toad and newt and viper;
And people call me the Pied Piper."

Into the street the Piper stept,

Smiling first a little smile,

As if he knew what magic slept

In his quiet pipe the while;

Then, like a musical adept,

To blow the pipe his lips he wrinkled,

And green and blue his sharp eyes twinkled,

Like a candle-flame where salt is sprinkled:

And ere three shrill notes the pipe uttered,

You heard as if an army muttered;

And the muttering grew to a grumbling;

And the grumbling grew to a mighty rumbling;

And out of the houses the rats came tumbling;

Great rats, small rats, lean rats, brawny rats,

Brown rats, black rats, grey rats, tawny rats,

Grave old plodders, gay young friskers,

Fathers, mothers, uncles, cousins,

Cocking tails, and pricking whiskers,

Families by tens and dozens;

Brothers, sisters, husbands, wives—

Followed the Piper for their lives.

From street to street he piped, advancing,

And step for step they followed dancing.

HOW THE WHALE GOT HIS THROAT

by Rudyard Kipling

In the sea, once upon a time, O my Best Beloved, there was a Whale, and he ate fishes. He ate the starfish and the garfish and the crab and the dab, and the plaice and the dace, and the skate and his mate, and the mackerel, and the pickereel, and the really, truly, twirly-whirly eel. All the fishes he could find in all the sea he ate with his mouth—so!

Then, on a raft, in the middle of the sea, with nothing to wear except a pair of blue canvas breeches, a pair of suspenders (you must particularly remember the suspenders, Best Beloved), and a jack-knife, he found one single, solitary, shipwrecked Mariner, trailing his toes in the water.

The Whale opened his mouth back and back and back till it nearly touched his tail, and he swallowed the ship-wrecked Mariner, and the raft he was sitting on, and his blue canvas breeches, and the suspenders (which you *must* not forget), *and* the jack-knife—he swallowed them all down into his warm, dark, inside cupboards, and then he smacked his lips—so, and turned round three times on his tail.

But as soon as the Mariner found himself truly inside the Whale's warm, dark, inside cupboards, he stumped and he jumped and he thumped and he bumped, and he pranced and he danced, and he banged and he clanged, and he hit and he bit, and he leaped and he creeped, and he prowled and he howled, and he hopped and he dropped, and he cried and he sighed, and he crawled and he bawled, and the Whale felt most unhappy indeed. (*Have* you forgotten the suspenders?)

So the Whale called down his throat to the ship-wrecked Mariner, "Come out and behave yourself. I've got the hiccoughs".

"Nay, nay!" said the Mariner. "Not so, but far otherwise. Take me to my native shore and the white-cliffs-of-Albion, and I'll think about it." And he began to dance more than ever.

So the Whale swam and swam and swam, with both flippers and his tail, as hard as he could for the hiccoughs; and at last he saw the Mariner's native shore and the white-cliffs-of-Albion. He rushed half-way up the beach, opened his mouth wide and wide and wide, and said, "Change here for Winchester, Ashuelot, Nashua, Keene, and stations on the *Fitch*burg Road". Just as he said "*Fitch*" the Mariner walked out of his mouth.

But while the whale had been swimming, the Mariner had taken his jack-knife and cut up the raft into a little square grating all running criss-cross, and he had tied it firm with his suspenders (*now* you know why you were not to forget the suspenders!) and he dragged that grating good and tight into the Whale's throat, and there it stuck! Then he recited the following *Sloka*, which, as you have not heard it, I will now proceed to relate—

> "*By means of a grating*
> *I have stopped your ating*".

The Mariner stepped out on the shingle and went home, married and lived happily ever afterwards. So did the Whale. But from that day on, the grating in his throat, which he could neither cough up nor swallow down, prevented him eating anything but very small fish; and that is the reason why whales nowadays never eat men or boys or little girls.

34

FROM A RAILWAY CARRIAGE

by Robert Louis Stevenson

Faster than fairies, faster than witches,

Bridges and houses, hedges and ditches;

And charging along like troops in a battle,

All through the meadows, the horses and cattle;

All of the sights of the hill and the plain

Fly as thick as driving rain;

And ever again, in the wink of an eye,

Painted stations whistle by.

Here is a child who clambers and scrambles,

All by himself and gathering brambles;

Here is a tramp who stands and gazes;

And there is the green for stringing the daisies!

Here is a cart run away in the road

Lumping along with man and load;

And here is a mill, and there is a river:

Each a glimpse and gone for ever!

SWALLOWS and AMAZONS

(By Arthur Ransome — Four children camp on an island. Their boat is named 'Swallow' and they have adventures with two other children in another boat called 'Amazon'. Here John, one of the boys, searches for a harbour in which to hide 'Swallow'.)

It was a little strip of beach curving round a tiny bay at the end of the island. A thick growth of hazels overhung it, and hid it from anyone who had not actually pushed his way through them. Beyond it the south-west corner of the island ran out nearly twenty yards into the water, a narrow rock seven or eight feet high, rising higher and then dropping gradually. Rocks sheltered it also from the south-east. There was a big rock that was part of the island, and then a chain of smaller ones beyond it. It was no wonder that they had thought that there was nothing but rocks there when they had sailed past outside.

"It may be only a puddle with no way into it," said John to himself.

He climbed out on to the top of the big rock. There was heather on the top of this rock, and John crawled out on it, looking down into the little pool below him. Further out on the far side of the pool he could see that there were big stones under water, but on this side it seemed clear. The water in there was perfectly smooth, because it was sheltered by the island itself from the wind which was still blowing lightly from the north-west. It looked as if you could bring a boat in from outside through a narrow channel between the rocks, but of course under water there might be rocks out there which he could not see. He climbed back and hurried to the camp.

"I've found the very place," he shouted.

The Charcoal Burners

(continued from ' Swallows and Amazons ')

On the other side of the clearing they found the track again. The noise of the chopping was now close at hand. A keen smell of smouldering wood tickled their nostrils. Suddenly they came out of the trees again on the open hillside. There were still plenty of larger trees, but the smaller ones and the undergrowth had been cut away. There were long piles of branches cut all of a length and neatly stacked, ready for the fire. There was one pile that made a complete circle with a hole in the middle of it. Forty or fifty yards away there was a great mound of earth with little jets of blue wood-smoke spirting from it. A man with a spade was patting the mound and putting a spadeful of earth wherever the smoke showed. Sometimes he climbed on the mound itself to smother a jet of smoke near the top of it. As soon as he closed one hole another jet of smoke would show itself somewhere else. The noise of chopping had stopped just before the explorers came into the open.

"Look, look," cried Titty.

At the edge of the wood, not far from the smoking mound, there was a hut shaped like a round tent, but made not of canvas but of larch poles set up on end and all sloping together so that the longer poles crossed each other at the top. On the side of it, nearest to the mound, there was a doorway covered with a hanging flap made of an old sack. The sack was pulled aside from within and a little old man, as wrinkled as a walnut and as brown, with long, bare arms, covered with muscles, came out. He blinked at the explorers in the sunlight.

"Hullo, you!" said the little old man.

It was very dark in the hut. The Swallows went in one by one and stood together inside the doorway. The old man had gone in first, but they could hardly see him. They heard him chuckle.

"You'll see better than bats in a minute. Sit down on yon bed."

Gradually their eyes grew accustomed to the darkness, and they saw that on each side of the hut a stout log divided off a place where there were rugs and blankets. Between the two logs there was an open space, where it looked as if there had been a small fire. The open light came through the doorhole. Not a speck of light came from between the poles of which the wigwam was made. Every chink had been well stuffed with moss. Overhead there hung a lantern from a hook at the end of a bit of wire. But it was not lit. High above them was pitch darkness, where the poles met each other at the pointed top of the hut. The old man was squatting on the log that shut off one of the bed-places. The Swallows sat in a row along the other.

"Do you live here while you're burning the charcoal?" asked Susan.

"Aye," said the old man. "Someone has to be with the fire night and day, to keep him down like."

"Have you really got a serpent?" asked Titty.

"An adder? Aye," said the old man. "Like to see him?"

"Oh yes, please," said all the Swallows.

"Well, you're sitting on him," said the old man.

All the Swallows jumped up as if they had sat on a pin. The old man laughed. He came across the hut and rummaged under the blanket and pulled out an old cigar box.

(The box belonged to young Billy, the old man's son.)

Young Billy put the box on the ground and knelt beside it. He undid the catch and lifted the lid. There was nothing to be seen but a lump of greenish moss. He took a twig and gently stirred the lump. There was a loud hiss, and the brown head of a snake shot out of the moss and over the side of the box. Its forked tongue darted in and out. Young Billy touched it gently with his twig. It hissed again and suddenly seemed to pour itself in a long, brown stream over the edge of the box. Young Billy dropped his twig and took a stick and picked the snake up on the stick and lifted it off the ground. Its tail hung down on one side of the stick and its head on the other. Its head swayed from side to side as it swung there, hissing and darting out its tongue. The Swallows shrank back from it but could not look away. Suddenly it began sliding over the stick. Young Billy was ready for it, and before it dropped on the ground he caught it on another stick.

"Is it safe to touch it?" asked Susan.

"Look," said young Billy. He lowered the snake to the ground and put the stick in front of it. Instantly the snake struck at it open-mouthed.

"Never you go near an adder," said young Billy. "There's plenty of them about. And you mind where you're stepping in the woods or up on the fell. They'll get out of your way if they see you, but if you happen to step on one, he'll bite, just as he did that stick. A bad bite it is too. There's many a one has died of it."

"What do you keep him for?" asked John.

"Luck," said young Billy.

44

NORDY BANK

by Sheena Porter

THE GREY ALSATIAN

The sun shining full in at the carriage windows was hot, without the wind that went with it. The luggage van was hot, too, and airless, particularly full because of the extra travellers and extra mailbags that went with Easter time. The guard was cross. Hadn't he got enough on his hands without that great alsatian sitting there staring at him? Savage brute snarled every time he walked past it. If it hadn't been muzzled, he reckoned his legs would have been in ribbons by now.

The alsatian was a young dog, with fine intelligent eyes, and a thick coat of wolf-grey fur brindled with black on the flanks. He snarled because he felt the guard's fear, because he was himself confused by the strangeness of his surrounding, and because his was a trained ferocity. He was an army dog.

The train rattled on: down between the Stretton hills and past the big yards of the sheep market at Craven Arms, down by Stokesay Castle and the racecourse at Bromfield, towards Ludlow. The alsatian, tethered by a thick leather leash between mail-bags and piled boxes of yellow chickens, laid back his ears and snarled silently. He was irritated by the loud and continuous cheeping of the chicks, as well as bewildered by the noise and movement of the train.

There was a sudden hiss of brakes and each carriage lurched backwards in turn, jostled by the buffer of the one before. The train shuddered to an unscheduled halt in Ludlow station. Mail-bags tumbled down on to their sides, and an enormous trunk slid heavily from one end of the van to the other. The guard opened the door.

"What the heck's the matter?" said the guard, seeing the station master running along the platform towards him. Two porters followed, pulling a large cart loaded with wooden boxes.

"Shan't keep you long," panted the station-master. "It's an SOS job. Bristol hospital wants this machine urgently. Been made here at Stackham's and rushed through the tests overnight. Are you full?"

"Yes, I am!" snapped the guard. "Hardly room to breathe in here as it is. Well, come on then. Let's get it all shifted round."

The first thing to be shifted was the alsatian. The guard reluctantly unstrapped the leash from the iron bars at the end of the van, and tried to pull the dog to one side out of the way. At that moment a porter stumbled against the piled boxes of chicks, which slithered and banged down on to the floor.

The alsatian pulled forwards; the guard stepped backwards; the leash flew out of his hand and the dog was gone. Some seconds had passed before the four men managed to make their way to the door, climbing over luggage and trying to avoid stepping on the chickens which had escaped from one of the boxes.

There was no one on the platform, because no train was due. There was no sign of the dog.

Away from the noise of the train and the noise of the town, where a track turned across open fields, the muzzled, grey alsatian ran steadily on into the countryside.

(To follow the adventures of the alsatian and to learn how he was rescued and tamed you must read the book. ' Nordy Bank ' won the Carnegie Medal for 1964. This award is given annually to an outstanding book for children.)

THE BOY'S SONG
by James Hogg

Where the pools are bright and deep,
Where the grey trout lies asleep,
Up the river and over the lea—
That's the way for Billy and me.

Where the blackbird sings the latest,
Where the hawthorn blooms the sweetest,
Where the nestlings chirp and flee—
That's the way for Billy and me.

Where the mowers mow the cleanest,
Where the hay lies thick and greenest,
There to track the homeward bee—
That's the way for Billy and me.

Where the hazel bank is steepest,
Where the shadow falls the deepest,
Where the clustering nuts fall free—
That's the way for Billy and me.

But this I know, I love to play,
Through the meadow, among the hay,
Up the water, and over the lea—
That's the way for Billy and me.

Learning by sounds

If children learn the sounds of letters and how to
blend them with the other letter sounds
(eg. c-a-t) they can tackle new words
independently (eg. P-a-t).

In the initial stages it is best if these phonic
words are already known to the learner.

However, not all English words can be learned
in this way as the English language is not purely
phonetic (eg. t-h-e).

In general a 'mixed' approach to reading is
recommended. Some words are learned by
blending the sounds of their letters and others
by look-and-say, whole word or sentence
methods.